Special Thanks to all the participants in DCFW!

Ean Williams, Derrick Rutledge, Guy Lambert, Alexis Zurdo, John Waller, Ronald Byrd, Yana Ziolkowski, Diara Nicole, Derrick Cox, Dr. Bo Best, Starbrille Cooper, and Gabrielle for cooperation and interviews, statements, and comments.

We appreciate your responses to our questions and aiding us in coverage of all four events this winter 2022.

Our Magazine has featured as many designs as possible, and we will be posting downloads on our site as well as links to how to purchase copies.

Issue no. 4 has been added, as well as alternative covers, as so many great designs warranted it. But will formally conclude our coverage here in this purely Pictoral issue.

They say a picture is worth a thousand words, so here are 51 photos by Harry Cee.

EXIT

GENERATION
GENERATION
GENERATION
GENERATION

www.ingramcontent.com/pod-product-compliance
Lightning Source LLC
Chambersburg PA
CBHW040154240726
48664CB00002B/692